The Tribe ot the Quraysh

SHAZIA NAZLEE

ILLUSTRATED BY ACHLA ANAND & ACHAL K. ANAND

Goodwordkidz

Goodword Books Pvt. Ltd.
1, Nizamuddin West Market, New Delhi 110 013
Tel. 435 5454, 435 6666 Fax 435 7333, 435 7980 E-mail: info@goodwordbooks.com

Makkah today, in the 21st century, is a large, modern city with high buildings, roads, street lamps and all the other things needed for daily living.

But in the time of the Prophet Muhammad ﷺ, Makkah was in the middle of a very hot desert, without roads, plants, restaurants, hotels, etc. However, the city did have a very blessed and important thing—the Ka'bah.

In Makkah, the most important tribe—the one to which the Prophet belonged—was called the Quraysh.

A proud people, they said, "No, never!" to the Prophet Muhammad ﷺ when he begged them to change their ways and give up their age-old religion for the sake of Islam.

Despite their hatred of Islam,
the Quraysh tribe were not at
all mean or narrow-minded.

They were known to be
good to their guests,
especially those who came
on the pilgrimage.

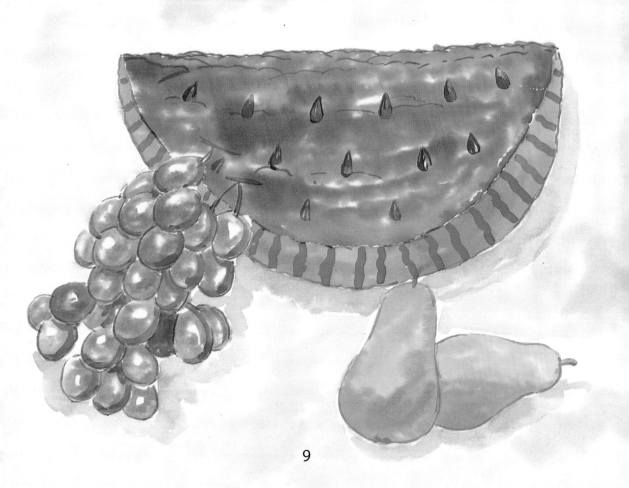

Even though the Quraysh tribe hated the Prophet ﷺ and rejected his message, Allah had still given them easier and better lives than others.

One great thing was that the Prophet had been sent especially to them. Then they were the keepers of the Ka'bah—a very important position.

Another blessing they had was the
water of the spring called Zamzam.

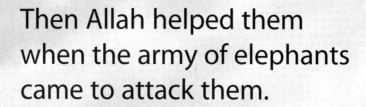

Then Allah helped them
when the army of elephants
came to attack them.

The city became very rich through trade and visitors to the Ka'bah. The Quraysh were known to be kind and to treat their guests well, so they were greatly respected by the traders and pilgrims.

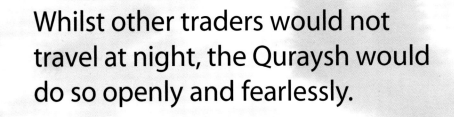

Whilst other traders would not travel at night, the Quraysh would do so openly and fearlessly.

20

Surah 106 of the Quran was revealed about the
Quraysh. In this, Allah reminds them that it was He
who blessed them with these great benefits, and
that they should turn to Him and worship Him
alone and be grateful to Him for what they had.

Surah Quraysh

For the benefit of the Quraysh.

For their benefit the caravans go out in the winter and summer.

So they should worship the Lord of this House.

Who has fed them, protected them from hunger, and has made them safer from fear.